PHILIPPINE FOLK FICTION
AND TALES

by

Teresita Veloso Pil

NEW DAY PUBLISHERS
877 Epifanio de los Santos
Quezon City

Illustrations: Norman Robles Garibay

ublishers Association of the Philippines, Inc.
Authorized under PCPM Certificate of Registration
SP No. 379

TABLE OF CONTENTS

FOLK FICTION

IFUGAO TALES

OTHER REGIONAL TALES

I. FOLK FICTION*

1. THE DRUM THAT RAN AWAY

2. AMIYAO AND HIS MAGIC GONGS

3. THE SOUL-TWIN TREE

4. THE BETEL TREE THAT WANTED TO BE A
   CHRISTMAS TREE

5. THE ANT'S JOURNEY

6. THE BELL NOBODY WANTED

A term probably used for the first time here to cover such tales as have been created in the imagination of a current writer, based on some tradition or more of a people. In time, such folk fiction may pass into the realm of the folktale.

THE DRUM THAT RAN AWAY

A story of the Ifugaos, a Philippine cultural minority group in the mountains of northern Luzon.

Dipdippo was an Ifugao drum that belonged to a powerful *mumbaki* or "priest-healer," an old man named Oltagon. Oltagon was also the village rice-chief whose duty it was to tend the *panon-acan*, a special ricefield which was, season after rice-season, always the first to be harvested in the whole village. It was taboo to plant or harvest any ricefield before the rice-chief had finished his; otherwise, the gods were certain to send rats or other pests to destroy the crops of the villagers.

Only a rice-chief could own a drum and ever since Dipdippo could remember, he was Oltagon's drum. Every harvest time, from the panon-acan, Dipdippo roared out his loud and resonant voice,

DIP-DIPPO, DIP-DIPPO, DIP-DIPPOOOOOOOO!

over the terraced fields that were hewn from the mountain-sides, across the falls that watered the mountain springs and into the villages to inform the people that Oltagon was starting his harvest. Dipdippo's call was also an invitation to all the villagers to attend the rice-harvest feast which Oltagon never failed to celebrate every harvest time.

Dipdippo remembered the many harvest feasts for which he had sung. Always the mumbakis danced around the sacrificial pigs that were offered to the harvest gods. Some of the priests twirled and hurled spears to drive away the jealous and harmful spirits; some swung colorful Ifugao blankets to drive away the rains and welcome the gentle winds; while others held ritual drinking bowls to splash rice-wine on the pigs and spread their benediction.

1

How Dipdippo loved those harvest-feasts! It was during those feasts when he could use the full range of his voice and sing most of his songs!

He always began with a gentle melody for the Invitation rite when Oltagon sang his special invitation song to a betelnut which was a magic one that Oltagon sent winging up to the sky regions to converse with the gods. Ever so softly, Dipdippo would sing, "Tup-pitti-tup, tup-pitti-tup, pitti-tup" while Oltagon intoned::

> It is up to you, Betel;
> This is your mission, Betel;
> Go up to the Skyworld and invite the deities:
> The Thunderer and the Earthquaker,
> The Sun, the Moon, and the Star-deities,
> And tell them to hasten to Oltagon's feast.

Then the other priests would join in to Dipdippo's louder tones:

> So that the rice may grow!
> So they may live in plenty, Oltagon and his kin!
> And their wealthiness be talked about
> In the villages throughout the earth-world!

For the dances that followed, Dipdippo always sang a merry tune:

> Tara-duk, duk, duk!   Tara-duk, ta-duk, ta-duk!
> Tara-duk, duk, duk!   Tara-duk, ta-duk, ta-duk!

And when the dancing priests were possessed by the gods or other spirits and began to dance frenziedly around the granary, Dipdippo would roar like the Thunder-god himself:

> BOOM – PAH – PAH – BOOM! PAH – PAH – BOOOMMM!

Dipdippo's sweetest song was reserved for the end of the harvest-feast rites when Oltagon would chant the magic tale of how rice was brought by the first ancestors from the skyworld to the earth. Oh, how he loved to listen to this story and because he did not want to miss a word, he sang in the barest whisper,

> Pim-pam, pim-pam-pam
> Pim-pam, pim-pam-pam

while Oltagon began his tale:

THE ORIGIN OF IFUGAO RICE

Once, when Kabbigat and his brother Ballitok were hunting, they espied a big wild pig and gave it chase.

Pim-pam, pim-pam-pam.

But the pig was a wily one and led the brothers in a long, merry chase around the earth-forest. Finally, looking for some means of escape, it climbed a lofty mountain peak where it jumped so high it landed in the skyworld itself. In hot pursuit, the two brothers did likewise.

Pim-pam, pim-pam-pam.

At last, on a rice-dike, the two brothers caught up with the pig and speared it on the spot. Suddenly, all the skygods seemed to appear, running towards the two, shouting angry threats.

"You have killed our pig and for this you two shall be punished severely! "

Kabbigat and Ballitok stood their ground, unafraid.

"This is a pig from earth which we followed to your place."

Amidst the babble of arguments, Bugan, the goddess of rice, on whose ricefield they were all converged, finally said:

"Wait, I will go and count our pigs and if their number has not decreased, then what these men say is true."

She left and came back soon after, smiling. "Our pigs are all there. These men are telling the truth."

At this point, Dipdippo raised his voice to a triumphant crescendo. He loved his heroes to win!

PIM-PAM, PIM — PAM — PAMMMMMMMMMMM!

So the two brothers cut up the meat, placed the pieces inside large green bamboo tubes and requested for fire in order to cook them. To their surprise, the gods replied:

"We have no fire. We always eat our food raw."

Kabbigat and Ballitok rubbed two dried bamboo sticks and built a fire. When the meat was cooked, they invited the gods to eat.

All the gods marvelled at the tasty flavor of the cooked meat. On the other hand, the two earthlings were delighted about the delicious white seeds that had stuck to the meat. They were told these were rice.

Before the brothers returned to earth, they gave fire to the gods in return for which they received the precious rice seedlings to plant on earth. Ever since that time, the Ifugaos have had rice to eat.

PIM — PAM, PIM-PAM-PAMMMMMMMM!

It was for a very special rite that Dipdippo sang his loudest song and he used his utmost strength to perform it. This he never sang at feasts for it had a powerful melody that he and Oltagon used only for great emergencies such as to stop a storm.

In their village, storms were of two kinds. One brought the winds that only felled the rice plants but did not destroy the pods. The other was more destructive and carried winds that stole the soul of the rice and left them dead. For this one Dipdippo's powerful song was used:

KA-BUUG! KA-KA-KA-BUUG, BUUG, BUUGGGGGG! ! !

No other drum sang that song. No other drum could stop a storm. No other drum had such magic!

Because of this, Dipdippo was regarded with much awe by the villagers. For the same reason, he was much coveted by the other villages. Many times he was stolen and carried away to distant villages but he always managed to run away from his captors and later be brought back to his own village by men who recognized him as Oltagon's drum.

Such incidents earned for Dipdippo the nickname "Drum-Who-Runs-Away," but when one of his captors fell ill and another's granary caught fire and it was rumored that these were caused by the drum, nobody dared to steal Dipdippo anymore. And so he stayed with Oltagon whom he loved very dearly.

There was one other person whom Dipdippo loved very much and he was Batullon, the grandson of Oltagon. Batullon was only a boy of nine years but already he knew by heart all the prayers, chants and rites of his tribal religion. Everyone in the village knew that someday Batullon would make a fine mumbaki like his grandfather, if his grandfather had his way. But there was Dulnuan, Batullon's father, who had other plans for the boy.

Dulnuan was in a hospital in the lowlands working his way to be a male nurse. He had aspired to be a doctor — white man's magic, Oltagon had called it — to help his people combat sickness and death which yearly took away many of his tribesmen.

Oltagon could very well have financed his son's medical education for he was a *kadangyan,* a rich man who owned many ricelands and several carabaos and pigs. But Oltagon had not offered help. It was not that he did not want to help, for a father has his duties to his children, but what Oltagon could not understand was why his own son chose to learn the practice of healing from total strangers in the lowlands when he, Oltagon, was a famous mumbaki.

"Have I not cured Kadangyan Ampupug, the great village chief, who lay dying for months because his soul had wandered off from his body? And did I not cure his crazy son from the evil spirits that had infested his mind? " Oltagon could go on and on citing his many achievements, for his fame as a priest and healer had spread far and wide to many villages.

But Dulnuan had only countered: "Were you able to save mother from death when she gave birth to me? And where was your famed magic when Inuki, my lovely wife, only 16 years old, died in giving life to my son, Batullon?"

Oltagon's face darkened with pain. "There are many instances when no power on earth can save a life. When the gods want you to die, you die. Even your white magicians know that," he replied.

"And there were as many instances when they could have been saved," Dulnuan argued doggedly. "And our gods have nothing to do with the cures. It is modern medicine and expert medical know-how."

How could Dulnuan say that? Oltagon knew — and how well he knew it—that if one did not offer a chicken or pig to the gods, a sick person would never get well. How could his son say this knowing his gods?

"Our healing rites are time-honored and our ancestors have practised them as taught to them by our gods."

"But our gods are not infallible!"

The quarrel between father and son had been bitter, and in the end, Dulnuan had left for the lowlands without his father's blessings. He also left behind his infant son, promising to return for him when it was time to start the boy's education.

That time had come and now Dulnuan was back in the mountain village to take his son with him to the lowlands.

A long argument ensued between Oltagon and his son for the old man was as determined to make Batullon a mumbaki, a tradition which for generations back had been the practice of all his male ancestors, as Dulnuan was adamant about his son's getting an education from the lowland schools.

In the end, Oltagon and Dulnuan compromised. Batullon was to go with his father to the lowlands, but on his thirteenth birthday, he was to return to his grandfather in order to become a mumbaki.

And so, Batullon bade his grandfather goodbye. He thought his heart would break and he wished Oltagon would change his mind and ask him to stay. But the old man had only said: "Take Dipdippo with you. When you get homesick and lonely, let him sing and it will seem as if you were back here in your mountain-home among your own people."

PART II

In the lowlands, Dipdippo was miserable. He longed for the cool mountains and the familiar faces of the people he loved. And he missed Oltagon very much.

In the first few months when both of them were new in the lowlands, Batullon sought the company of Dipdippo very often. Together they would sing of the mountains which evoked familiar scenes that seemed to transport them back to their beloved village. But later, Batullon became busy with school and books and new-found friends and Dipdippo was left pretty much alone most of the time.

One day, Batullon took the drum from its dusty shelf.

"Teacher wants me to show my school-friends our dances. They want to know more about our people. Will you join me? " he asked the drum.

Dipdippo had never seen a formal classroom. He thought it was like the under-yard of the rice granaries where the young boys who aspired to be priests learned the rites and prayers by sitting close to the mumbakis during actual ceremonies.

"Let's do the Spear Dance Rite! " Dipdippo was excited as he hummed a tune.

The program turned out to be a humiliating experience for both Batullon and Dipdippo. To many in the audience of school children,

Batullon's performance was strange and crude and they laughed at the near-nakedness of the boy who, for the occasion, had worn the G-string costume that had been the attire of his people for centuries.

As for Dipdippo, he got the beating of his life for the boy who played the drum used two hard sticks with much gusto, unaware that Ifugao drums are always played with the bare hands.

Batullon took his drum and fled to their house where he unashamedly cried out his humiliation. When Dulnuan returned from the hospital, Batullon begged to be allowed to return to the mountains and to Oltagon.

"I can't go back to school after what happened! " the boy cried.

But Dulnuan had gone through similar experiences before and, quietly, he told his son: "It takes a long time for people to accept other people with different beliefs and customs from theirs. They will, later on, when they find out you are just as good as they are. That is what we will have to prove to them."

But the boy sobbed on, seemingly inconsolable.

"Remember when I returned to our mountain village the first time? " asked Dulnuan.

Batullon had heard about it from the older folks.

"Your own uncles laughed at me for wearing the clothes of the lowlander. They jeered at me for covering my legs with long pants and at every opportunity they would scoffingly ask if I was ashamed to bare my chest as I used to do in the mountains."

Batullon's sobs ceased.

"Later, they realized that the strange clothes I wore did not make me any less Ifugao than they. When they understood this, they took me back into their hearts."

Batullon stayed and returned to school. On some days, he would bring along the drum for his teachers had asked him to teach them his songs. Later, he and Dipdippo taught the dances and, in turn, they learned the dances of the lowlands.

But the drum was not happy. Yet he could not understand why for he had found new friends and the children had begun to love him.

One day, a relative came with the news that Oltagon was gravely ill. Dulnuan, Batullon and the drum almost flew through the mountain roads and trails that led back to their village.

When they arrived, they thought they were too late, but Oltagon opened his eyes, held Dulnuan's hands with his own weak ones, and said in a voice barely above a whisper:

"Take the lands . . . the granaries . . . the carabaos. Be a good doctor . . . and come back . . . cure your people . . . "

He looked lovingly at Batullon and continued: "Learn well . . . from your father . . . ."

Then he turned to Dipdippo and gave his faithful friend three loving taps on the head. It was the last time Dipdippo was to sing for his beloved master. "And it is the last time I will sing, ever," thought the drum, for he secretly planned to follow his beloved master.

Oltagon's body, garbed in the habiliments of the rich kadangyan, was placed on the *haludag,* or death chair, under his house while his relatives sang the *alim* citing his great achievements as a revered mumbaki. Dipdippo stood mute and silent beside him.

Outside, in the side-yard of the house, people were dancing to the beat of several gongs while a few yards away ten carabaos and an equal number of pigs were being butchered. The dancing, the gong-playing and the carabaos and the pigs were part of the ceremonial to properly send Oltagon's spirit to the land of the souls where his ancestors had gone before him.

After Oltagon was buried inside the great mountain cave where all the tribal greats were interred, Dipdippo made his own plans to join him in the spirit-world in the sky.

That night, after Dulnuan and Batullon had finally fallen asleep, much fatigued from the long ceremonies of the past three days, Dipdippo ran away. Down mountainsides and cliffs, down terraced walls he rolled until he found himself in an abandoned panon-acan. Its stone-walls had crumpled long ago when a huge landslide had rumbled down the mountain and had, since then, been left to time and the elements.

The drum sank against the soft mud and went to sleep. The next morning, he was awakened by the sun just as it climbed above the mountain-tops.

Then he heard it. At first it was only a faint call, but louder and louder, it came.

Dip-dippooooo! DIP-DIPPOOOO! COME BACK! ! ! ! !

It was Batullon who had come to look for him. The people who heard the boy's call remarked: "That drum has run away again! "

Then the boy was suddenly there, right in front of him!

"He mustn't see me! " Dipdippo thought frantically and sank a little deeper in the mud, remaining motionless.

Batullon stared hard and long at the spot where the drum was. He was certain that he saw the elaborate markings on its side that his grandfather had carved long ago. But when he looked again it was gone. Batullon thought his eyes were playing tricks on him and he went further on.

The drum felt very sad for the boy and almost called to him. But then he remembered that Batullon and his father were soon returning to the lowlands, back to their studies. He whispered back: "No, Batullon, I can't go back with you. I belong to your grandfather, he and I belong to another time."

Then he remembered the great harvest-feasts of Oltagon. How he had sung at those feasts! And how the mumbakis had danced to his music! They all seemed to be there now, dancing right before his very eyes!

Then the scene shifted and he saw him with Batullon in a lowland school-house, teaching children to dance the mountain dances. Although the scene was a happy one, he saw an unhappy drum. He compared the scene with that of the harvest feast and he began to under stand at last why he had been sad and unhappy in the school-house scene even when he had come to love the children.

What Dipdippo realized was that he was a sacred ritual drum who was truly happy only in the highlands, among the terraced ricefields and the rice-plants that he had helped to raise and make grow with his songs.

Batullon's call grew fainter and fainter until only the echoes floated back to the drum. Dipdippo sank deeper still into the soft mire until he could hear the echoes no more. "Drum-Who-Runs-Away" had run away for the last time.

AMIYAO AND HIS MAGIC GONGS

Gongs are in general use among the mountain tribes which dwell in Northern Luzon. They are used to accompany dances and are played during religious rites and ceremonies. Traditionally, they are owned only by the rich and constitute one of the symbols of their wealth.

Many mountain peoples attribute divine origin to their gongs. The Tinguians, for example, believe that their god Kabunian gave mankind expensive porcelain jars and gongs and a tree which bore agate beads, rice, rice-wine, sugarcane, etc. The story below is woven around that belief.

Amiyao was a Tinguian boy of fourteen who lived with his widowed mother and a younger sister aged ten years. Since his father was dead, Amiyao was his mother's great helper in the work on their small ricefield, camote and vegetable patch, and, during the months after the harvest when the ricelands were idle, in the hunt for deer and wild pig.

The village where Amiyao lived was a poor one. They did not produce enough rice to last until the next harvest, so the people had to supplement their diet with camotes and vegetables. It seemed to Amiyao that the villagers worked very hard from sun-up to sun-down and enjoyed no rest. There seemed to be nothing to break the humdrum day-to-day monotony, no high points in their lives that the villagers could celebrate and remember with beautiful memories.

Once, in one of his hunting forays away from his village, a shift of wind brought strange sounds to his ears. Curious, Amiyao sought the source of the strange sounds and soon came upon a village in riotous celebration of a feast. People, young and old, were dancing happily to the sounds of circular bells which were played by young men who were also dancing.

"Bang-ba-lang-bang, ba-lang-bang! " one of the gongs sang.

"Butegig, butegig, bu-te-ggiggg! " answered another.

"Tung-tung-tang! Tung-tung-tang! " a smaller gong fairly shouted while a fourth one, its high-pitched voice barely audible above the louder and bigger gongs, joined in the chorus: "Ting-ting-ohhh! Ting-ting-ohhh! "

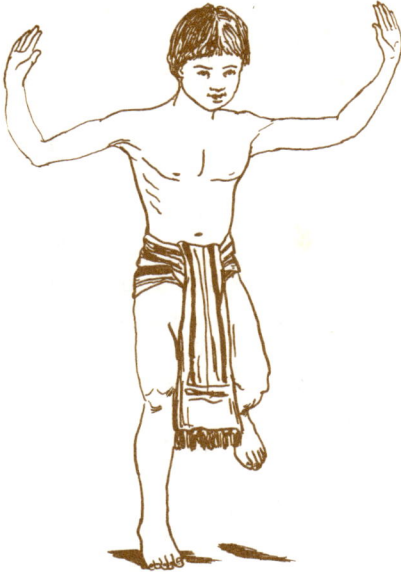

Amiyao listened, fascinated. And such was the compelling magic of the gongs that he soon found himself executing an unfamiliar jig! A step forward, a hop, a turn and all the time his arms were flapping, like the wings of a bird in flight, in perfect time to the music! Amiyao flushed with pleasure, enjoying his dance immensely. He had never danced before but he knew that the magic gongs had given him the power to move in harmonious rhythm. Now he understood why his villagers never danced nor held feasts. There were no magic gongs in their village to give them the power of rhythmic and harmonious movement!

When Amiyao returned to his village he could not forget the music of the gongs. He remembered their magic melody that made people dance happily.

One day, he gathered enough courage to ask the village elders where he could get the magic gongs but some of them just shook their heads sadly while others said that the gongs came from far away, across the seas. Finally, a wise old priest told Amiyao that the gongs belonged to Kabunian, the benevolent Skyworld god who made the earth.

"Long ago," the old priest said, "our village had these magic musical instruments and there were many days of feasting and dancing. But one day, Kabunian was displeased when people forgot to offer him sacrifices. In anger, he took back the gongs and hid them deep down in the bowels of the mountain." the old priest looked intently at the young boy and continued, "They are still there, imprisoned, until some brave young man brings them back to our impoverished village."

For a long time, Amiyao thought about the words of the old priest. Deep in his heart he believed the old priest was challenging him to undertake the mission.

One day, as he was hunting in the mountains for a wild pig, he lost his way. He looked at the sky and discovered that the sun was already half-way between noon and evening. He had to hurry and find his way before darkness covered the safe mountain trails.

Suddenly, he espied a wild pig. It was an albino seldom seen in this part of the mountains. A village legend had it that the man who sighted one of these white pigs was very lucky indeed for the gods were said to rain down abundant blessings on him ever after.

In a flash, the boy was after the pig. Through thicket and brush and rocks which cut through his skin, Amiyao refused to let the disappearing animal out of his sight, but every time he thought he had the pig, he would suddenly find it out of his reach again. Soon, he saw the pig disappear into a mountain wall. Upon closer examination, Amiyao found an entrance in the wall behind a rock ledge, which led to a cave. In the darkness, Amiyao slowly made his way inside, forgetting that danger might lie ahead. All he wanted was to catch the pig to ensure the blessings of the gods on his village and himself.

Finally, he saw a light and, going towards it, found he was in the deepest part of the cave; the light came from a very large tall tree that stood in the middle of the cave. The tree was laden with gongs, rice, gold and silver jewelry and other paraphernalia used only by the wealthy. Unafraid, Amiyao approached the tree and slowly reached

for one gold necklace. He placed it around his neck and it seemed to belong there. Then he put on some gold earrings, silver armlets and copper leglets and lo! he looked every inch like a handsome young chief! Then he took down four gongs, each bigger than the other. When he played on them, his ears tingled with pleasure their sound was pure and strong!

Amiyao did not forget to bring some rice for his people. When he finally returned to his village, he sounded his gongs throughout his journey, and their melodious notes filled the mountainside and reverberated through the villages. All the people ran to welcome Amiyao. They made him their chief and there was merrymaking, feasting and dancing that lasted for several days.

From that time on, their village prospered, for Amiyao was a wise and kind ruler who taught his people industry. The harvest became bountiful and the people were happy.

And the gongs stayed with Amiyao and his people for he never forgot to thank the gods for their benevolent gifts by giving feasts and dances in their honor.

THE SOUL-TWIN TREE

High up in the mountains of northern Luzon, Philippines, certain tribes hold the belief that a tree must be planted when a child is born. This tree is called the child's Soul-Twin and the legend goes that as the tree lives so shall the child; if it withers and dies, so shall the child sicken and die, for, according to belief, what happens to one is sure to have a similar effect on the other. Why the people hold such a belief may be explained by the fact that mountain life is harsh and the future uncertain, and the tree is one of their means of lessening the uncertainties.

When Bugan-nak-Amtalao (Bugan, child of Amtalao) was born, her parents planted for her her very own soul-twin. It was a sapling of a narra tree, one of those beautiful and sturdy hardwoods that thrive in the forests of Bontoc. As the tree grew, Bugan's parents could already see how beautiful and strong Bugan would be when she grew up.

Like a true mountaineer, Bugan learned to take care of her tree when she was quite young. She named it Bugan-nak-Amtalao-Little-Tree and every day she would bring it water to drink, calling in her sweet sing-song voice: "Bugan-nak-Amtalao-Little-Tree, here is water for you, fresh from the spring. Drink it so you may grow tall and strong like your cousin-hood in the deep forests where my father, Amtalao, hunts."

On some mornings, Bugan the little girl would bring Bugan the tree some rice to eat. And when her father brought home deer and wild pig from the hunt, some pieces of the salted meat was sure to be added to the rice for Bugan the tree. And the tree would clap her leafy boughs in delight for although she could not eat the rice and meat herself she knew the birds would come to eat them, and how she loved to hear the birds a-chirping among her now sturdier branches! Many a time the mountains would echo with the happy voices of birds, tree and little girl at play. At times, even the mountain mists would join them in a fast game of hide-and-seek!

Of late, however, Bugan the tree would find herself alone in the mornings for Bugan the girl, now eight years old, began to accompany her mother to their small mountain clearing where they had planted sweet potatoes. It was located at some distance from their home and by the time the mother and child returned, it was well into the afternoon. But every time Bugan the girl returned she always had lots of wonderful stories to tell the tree of the things she had seen on the other side of the mountain. Oftentimes, she would sing the stories to the tree this way:

"Oh, Bugan-nak-Amtalao-Little-Tree,
Did you know there's a funny little monkey
        down at our camote clearing?
He is a robber, that fellow; he stole my basket
        of camotes
And   when I threw a stick at him,
He did the same to me! "

Or this story:

"Oh, Bugan-nak-Amtalao-Little-Tree,
Did you know there's a red pit-pit bird
        by the spring near our camote clearing?
He sang a little tune to me: 'Pit-pit-pit,'
But mother says that if he sings it another way
It is a bad omen."

And yet another one:

"Oh, Bugan-nak-Amtalao-Little-Tree,
Did you know there's a golden tree
        in the middle of the big forest?

When Mother and I passed along the high rice-terrace
      wall of Old Man Ampumpug,
I saw its golden leaves reflected in the sunlight.
Mother says that long, long ago, when my ancestors lived,
This very tree bore the agate beads and the gold earrings
      that our rich tribesmen now wear."

Many times the evening stars would already appear in the west before Bugan the girl could finish telling all her stories. And, oh, how the tree and the birds that now nested on her branches loved to hear the stories! And, oh, how they all loved the little girl who told them the many wonderful tales!

But one day, Bugan the little girl did not come out from her hut. Another day came and yet another, but she was nowhere to be seen. The tree and all the birds began to worry. Where was Bugan-nak-Amtalao-Little-Girl? Did she go away without telling them? Without even a goodbye?

But Bugan the little girl had not gone away. She was inside the hut lying feverish and ill. Several *mumbakis* or priests of their tribal religion came and offered sacrifices of pigs and chickens to the god Kabunian who lived in the Skyworld. But Bugan did not get well; in fact, she seemed to get worse. And the priests were all puzzled for the Soul-Twin tree showed no signs of withering or decay.

"Surely, it is one of your ancestors," the oldest *mumbaki* told Bugan's parents. "He is lonely up there in his abode in the Skyworld and wants some child to play with. We will have to give him a large pig so he will stop making Bugan sick."

So a much bigger pig was sacrificed to Amtalao, an ancestor of Bugan, who was suspected of causing her illness.

"Here, you ancestor Amtalao," the priest intoned solemnly. "Here is your pig. Do not get the soul of our beloved Bugan, but instead go back to your abode in the sky and play with the soul of this fat pig we are giving you."

But, in spite of all the offerings of pigs and chickens, Bugan-nak-Amtalao-Little-Girl wasted away.

One afternoon, when the sun was half-way to its setting place, a small procession started from Bugan's hut towards a mountain declivity where Bugan's ancestors were buried. As the procession passed by the tree, Bugan the tree gave out a sharp cry of pain, for, carried in a blanket-sling by her father Amtalao, was the lifeless body of her beloved Bugan. The wind carried the grief-stricken cry of the poor tree and as it raced across the tree-tops the whole mountainside seemed to mourn for the dead girl.

After that, Bugan the tree was never happy again. How she missed the little girl! No one came to sing to her anymore; no one came to tell her the wonderful stories of the outside world. No little girl came around anymore to swing on her branches and add her happy voice to the songs of the birds and the wind. No one came to bring her water and food, and soon her branches began to dry up and wither. The birds soon ceased to come for they had flown away to seek sturdier branches whereon to build their nests.

One night, Kolyog, the earthquake, came and moved the mountains. It sent soil and rocks hurtling down the mountainsides and made the big ancient trees shake in fright. The weak, sad tree, trembling to her very roots, gave a last sigh and fell headlong to the ground below.

The next morning, when Bugan's father looked out of the window, he saw the tree lying on the ground, its trunk uprooted. "Look! At last Little Bugan's tree has joined her in the Skyworld!"

THE BETEL TREE THAT WANTED TO BE A CHRISTMAS TREE

Once upon a mountain-top, there lived a small betel tree. She had betel-nut fruits that were Christmasy-red with their crowns tinged with gold. Because of this she wanted very much to be a Christmas tree to light up a home for Christmas.

Unfortunately, she had only four sparse and scrawny palm leaves. They could not even hold a Christmas candle, much less a Christmas star.

And so, season after Christmas season people just ignored the tree. They did not know her Christmasy-red-and-gold-tinged fruit could brighten up their homes more than a hundred candles could.

One Christmas season she had brighter hopes than ever. She felt that this time at last she would realize her dream for she had grown a foot taller and two palm-fronds had been added to the scrawny four. But the days passed and now it was already the 24th of December, and her hopes lay dim; nobody had taken her.

That night, as she looked up at the starry sky she saw that the sparkling stars had joined together and formed a huge Christmas tree across the great blue dome. "Even the lovely stars want to be Christmas trees, too! " she said sadly. "And here I am — a real tree with Christmasy fruits — and I can't even be one! "

Then she perked up for there at the tip of the star-made Christmas tree was the Fairy Star shining in all her brilliance. Her heart leapt with joyful hope for, according to a legend believed by all the trees on that mountain-top, when one saw the Fairy Star on a Christmas night, one's wish would come true.

"I wish to be a Christmas tree! I want to shine and hold a star on my head! " She closed her eyes and concentrated on her wish. Then she waited. But nothing happened.

"Fairy Star," she pleaded, "PLEASE make me a Christmas tree. Make me brighten people's hearts — even only for a season! "

She thought the Fairy Star winked at her. Then she waited for the magic — for the moment when her wish would come true. But it passed and nothing happened.

Then a tear fell and then another. Then they came in torrents and as the uncontrollable sobs grew greater, the red-and-gold-tinged fruits fell to the ground. Finally her sob ceased and she fell asleep.

Down from her starry heights the Fairy Star came to the tree. She saw the bright fruits on the ground. "Why, the poor little one has really broken her heart. I think I shall grant her wish."

The Fairy Star took the tree's scrawny fronds and wove each of them into cone-shaped hats. Then she gathered the red betel-nut fruits from the ground and attached them to the palm-cones with the fairy-gold threads that she had made from the tree's tears. On the top of the smallest palm-cone, the Fairy Star placed a brilliant star which she took from her own crown. It gave such a lovely light that the whole mountain-top glowed.

When the tree woke up she felt strangely happy and wondered why. She knew that she was the same old betel-nut tree that had only six scrawny palm-fronds which could not even hold a Christmas star. She looked for her red and gold fruits that had fallen to the ground but they were nowhere. Then she realized that the fruits were happily hanging from her branches which had magically become cone-shaped. She looked up and saw the golden star on her crown and its brilliance rivalled those of the stars in the sky!

Finally, she realized with great joy that her wish had come true — she had become a real Christmas tree!

THE ANT'S JOURNEY

In an anthill by a river that meandered along a golf course, lived Ametta, a tiny black ant. She belonged to the worker class of ants whose daily routine of work was seemingly unending. But this hard-working ant had a special dream other worker ants did not care about — she wanted to travel and see the world.

Now, worker ants do much travelling, of course. Through crooked pathways in the grass and among tangled roots, over stones and thick stalks of weeds, at times climbing over fallen trees and crossing deep gullies, they leave their ant-hill homes to go to the outside world in search of food.

But this sort of travel was not the kind that Ametta had set her heart on. Ground travel was very limiting—only a few hundred yards a day—and very tedious, particularly when one had to use one's own footpower. What she had in mind was air travel, especially to the moon. And here was the reason:

Once, she had taken a ride on a leaf. The trip wasn't planned; she just happened to be there when the leaf was leaving. It took Ametta several days to find out that she had not travelled very far, but the feel of air rushing past her ears and the exhilarating experience of being airborne was such an unforgettable one for her that she hastened to tell a skylark about it.

But the bird was not impressed. "Did you reach the skies? " the skylark asked haughtily.

"Have you? " countered the ant who disliked haughty people.

The skylark stood tall and held his head much higher. "My eminent ancestors are known to have flown so high that they banged their heads against the sky, singeing their hair. That is why we skylarks are bald today." And he proudly showed his bald pate to the ant.

"This mark distinguishes us skylarks from the less renowned birds and from the common LOWLY insects." He lingered on the word *lowly* and gave the ant an insolent stare.

But ants can also come up with a sting or two when provoked. Ametta answered, "If I had wings, I'd surely touch the stars and get a bit of their luster and not go banging my head against skies and getting a bald pate. That was a very stupid thing to do."

The skylark flew into a rage. "Why, you land-grub, you hill-dweller, you Ordinary Thing! " Skylark usually ran short of adjectives when he got into a high rage. "I dare you to go to the moon and come back to tell about it! " Skylark flew away in a din of angry wings, screaming: "I DARE YOU! I DARE YOU! "

The tiny ant, feelings ruffled but determined, shouted back: "I accept! I ACCEPT YOUR DARE! JUST YOU WAIT AND SEE! "

From then on, going to the moon occupied Ametta's dreams. At night, when the moon was high in the sky, she would climb to the roof of her ant-hill home to gaze at this majestic white ball. But, even from her high roof-top perch, the moon seemed very, very far away indeed. It was, Ametta admitted, a rather big task. But when she remembered again the skylark's insolence, she knew she had to do it.

And so, Ametta wove her dreams.

One day, she tried to borrow wings from the crow. She was a very well-travelled crow and wore the air of a cosmopolite. The crow always wore black because she said it was a mark of elegance.

"Black is beautiful, my deah. . ." Crow always dropped her R's every time she newly returned from her foreign sojourns. "It is a 'must' for formal evenings," she told Ametta. And she opened her wings, much like a high-fashion model does to display an expensive shawl, and strutted about.

However, Crow would not lend the ant her wings for she could not stand being grounded for long. In the summers, she had to fly north to escape the heat and in the winters, fly south to escape the northern cold. And in the springs and autumns, she had to be at other places to be with her other high-class friends. Crow could not remember what she and her rich friends were escaping from during these seasons but travelling was a pattern for them now.

The other fleet-winged birds could not spare their wings either, for they were busy birds who could not stay put in one place for long. Only the kind moth offered his wings but Ametta could not use them for they were too fragile for the long flight. So it seemed that Ametta was farther than ever from realizing her dreams.

One day, she found a golf ball. Only she did not know it was a golf ball. She thought it was the moon that had fallen from the sky. With great joy she climbed over to its rounded top.

Suddenly, a great whoozing sound came and WHACK! the ball and the ant were whisked off high into the air, up and up over the tall tree-tops they soared. Ametta was dizzy from the height, for she had never gone this far up, but she clung fiercely to what she thought was the moon.

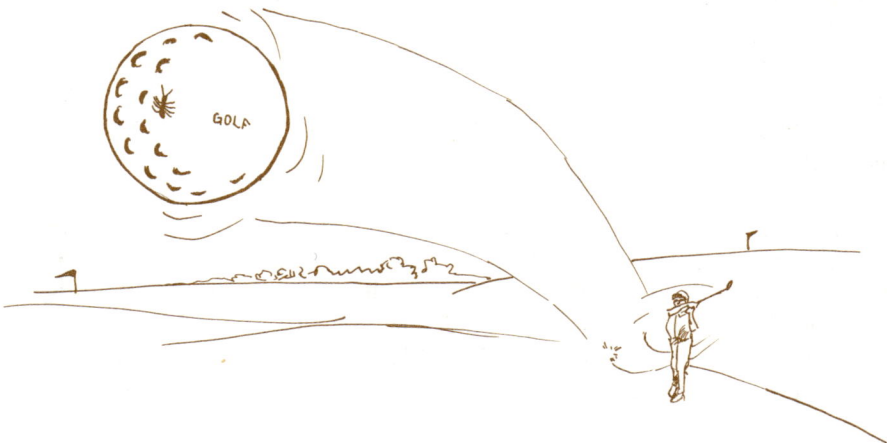

"Hah, that haughty lark should see me now! I am riding on the moon! " she sang exultantly, albeit a little dizzily.

All too soon they were descending and KERPLUNK! ball and ant landed on a green lawn and rolled on the soft grass and sank into a hole. The poor ant got a terrible beating and she remembered the sky-lark and his story about how his ancestors lost their hair. She felt her head and discovered a missing feeler.

"It must be that when you reach for high things like the moon or the sky you lose a part of yourself," she said sadly.

Soon she heard voices and a hand reached out for the ball. "A hole-in-one! I could kiss this ball! " A man's voice remarked in jest. Then the man saw the ant.

"Look, here's a tiny black ant on my golf ball! " He winked his eye in jest. "This is my good luck charm. I believe I shall bring it home with me." And there was laughter all around.

The lucky golfer did bring the ant home with him for it would not let go of the ball. It clung desperately to the ball for the ant believed it was the moon which she wanted to show off to the skylark.

The golfer placed the ball and the ant in a special place and gave the ant some honey. It was a very sad ant who learned that the ball was not the moon. As a matter of fact, the golfer had more balls in his study.

But all was not lost for Ametta; it turned out that the golfer was a scientist due to leave in a few days with other scientists for a space flight to observe animal behaviour in space. He was bringing along with him some small animals and a pair of canary birds.

"How would you like to come along with me to outer space, Ant? " the scientist asked. "Would you like that? "

Ametta waved her arms vigorously in approval and because she could not contain her happiness, she ran around in several circles. "It is fantastic how your wildest dreams sometimes come true! " she said in disbelief. "Wait till I tell the skylark about this! " she gloated. "Wait till I tell that insolent bird! "

In the space ship, they went up and up and up in ever increasing speed. Beyond the clouds, beyond the stars, even beyond the moon they seemed to soar! Ametta felt strange that she was looking right at them instead of up at them as she had often done on earth.

And they were beautiful! The stars were alive, blinking, twinkling, sparkling, incessantly shooting off lights in a thousand radiant colors. And the Milky Way was a giant necklace of pure silver stars that made a pathway across the sky as if millions of diamonds were strewn on a ribbon of gossamer silk.

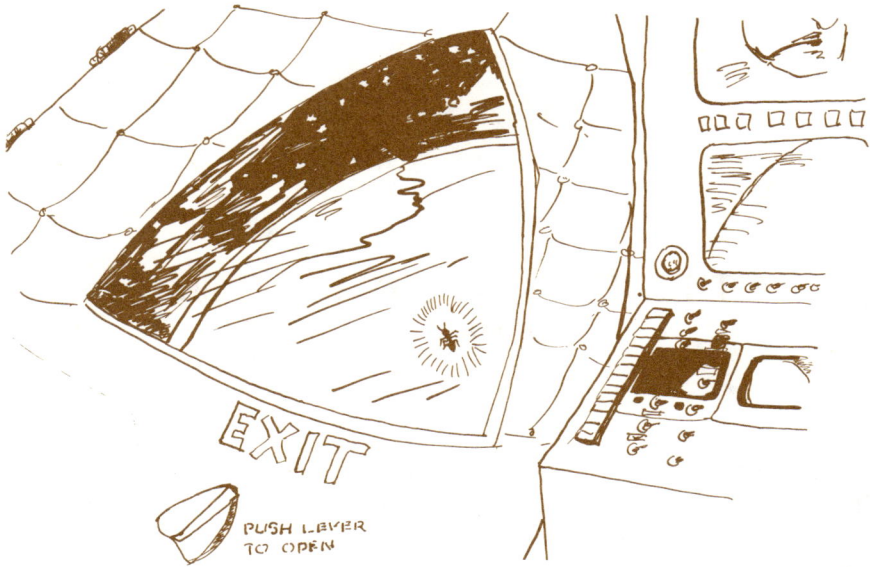

EXIT

PUSH LEVER
TO OPEN

The moon itself was a pinkish hue, like one forever blushing, as it reflected the light of the mighty red sun.

"How marvelous! Nothing on earth could compare with this!" Ametta exclaimed.

She looked down at the earth. It was only a brown blur in the distance. And as she looked, she thought she saw the skylark, now a tiny insignificant blot in that brown blur.

And whether it was the exhilaration of being so high up, or the perspective it gave her, all of a sudden Ametta felt the resentment she had against the skylark melt away as she realized that, after all, it was the skylark who had egged her on, who had driven her to seek greater heights — his had been the challenge that gave her the wings to fly!

In a new feeling of humility, Ametta blew a kiss across the miles to the skylark — "Thank you, thank you! I wish you were here to enjoy these lovely sights with me!"

THE BELL NOBODY WANTED

(A Christmas Story)

Far away, in a big city in the tropics, a huge cathedral was being built. The people wanted it to be beautiful and lasting and so they tried to get the best builders and the very best materials that could be found in the land.

When the cathedral was finished, invitations for the inaugural celebration were sent out, but, to the dismay of everyone, it was found that nobody had remembered to order the bells for the towering belfry. No less than a chime of 15 bells, each producing a different tone, was needed for such a huge belfry. Indeed, a grand carillon it had to be and this made everybody sad for they all thought that the inauguration would have to be celebrated without the bells. However, a hurried call to the silversmith assured everyone that work on the bells would be rushed and finished in time for the celebration. All the people heaved a sigh of relief.

At last the bells were ready. Many people watched the workmen operate the giant cranes that were to hoist the heavy carillon to the high tower. But as the workmen attached the bells to the crane's steel supports it was discovered that there was one bell too many! One little extra bell was found to be quite out of place in the carillon.

It was a silver bell, its edges scalloped like lace edgings, and at the points where the scallops joined, small stars were exquisitely outlined. At the top, near its handle, a miniature Star of Bethlehem was engraved, its points of light radiating towards the smaller stars.

"Harrumph! " grumbled one workman as he began to detach the little bell from the rest of the set, "some idiot at the smithy must have slept on his job."

He took hold of the tiny bell which did seem too fancy and fragile for the heavy work at the belfry, but it wriggled itself free and began to peal desperately. "Ting-a-ling-ling, ting-a-ling-ling! " it pleaded.

"Please don't take me away. I want to be with the other bells. I want to live up in the church's tower and sing to the world. I want to make people happy with my song!"

But the grumpy workman did not listen; in fact, he did not hear the bell's plea. Instead, he grabbed the bell and threw it to a fellow-worker. "Hey, take a look at this fancy bell," he said. "All decked out, like a Christmas tree! Hah!"

"But I am a Christmas bell," protested the little chimer. "Only I don't want to be useful for just one season; I want to make people happy the whole year round. That is why I want to be with the other bells in the tower so I can sing every day and make the people happy."

With a sinking heart, the little bell saw the other bells in the carillon now being hoisted by the huge cranes towards the high cathedral tower. Resolutely, it made a big jump towards the cranes but missed and fell headlong to the pavement below. Poor, poor little bell! A big crack opened its sides and when the other workman tried to make it peal, only a miserable "twang-a-langgg-langgg" came forth making him laugh derisively.

"Oh, come now. Throw that bell into that trash-can over there and let's go," the first workman said. "It's useless anyway. Nobody would want it now." And they both walked away.

The little bell's heart was literally broken. Now she could never sing in harmony with the other bells. Now she would never be allowed up the belfry to sing happily for all the world to hear. Now she could not even serve as a Christmas bell to ring and peal at Christmastime and be wrapped in soft tissue for the rest of the year. Instead here she was in a filthy garbage can! Oh, how bitterly she cried. And as she rolled in grief, her dismal little voice could be heard, "Twanggg-a-langgg-langgg!"

Sometime later, two garbage scroungers found the unhappy bell. "Say, this one could easily bring us three or even five pesos," one of them hopefully appraised the bell's value.

The bell perked up. At last, she thought, somebody needs me. But when the scroungers saw its big crack and heard its pathetic sound, they threw the bell back into the heap in plain disgust.

Meanwhile, in the poorer section of the city, an orphan boy of twelve, named Mario, was wearily pushing his ice-cream cart. The Christmas season had filled the stores and streets with shoppers and, anticipating brisker sales, the ice-cream company had accepted even the twelve-year-old Mario as a vendor.

However, Christmas notwithstanding, Mario's sales were very discouraging. Not because the weather had turned cold—for in Mario's country they had year-round sunshine—but because Mario had no bell and, as you and I know, this is standard equipment in selling ice-cream. The week before, Mario's bell had been stolen and he did not have enough money to buy another one immediately. So for the past several days he had had to shout his wares.

"If only I had my bell back," he wished hard. Then, as if addressing Somebody Up There, he looked heavenwards and repeated: "Please, I wish I had my bell back."

Then he saw this cross, all aglow in the distance, as if suspended from the clouds. At that moment, the bells began to ring and the sound of firecrackers rent the air. "Oooh," he smiled with pleasure, "it must be the inauguration of that new church they have been talking about." With hurrying feet he sped towards the place where the new cathedral stood.

The church's facade was ablaze with a million lights and there were many, many people around. Out of the huge front doors a procession was emerging and Mario pressed forward to get a good look. But the crowd was too thick and he was too small so he climbed aboard his cart to get a better view. Suddenly, the cart was roughly shoved back and, to his chagrin, he and his ice-cream cart were soon careening towards a fence-wall where a garbage can stood.

"Twangg-a-langg-lang, twang-a-lang-langgg!" Something fell from the overturned heap-can and rolled towards him. It was a small bell, dirty with grime and an ugly crack on its side that marred its engraving of stars. But to Mario it was the most beautiful thing in the world. His heart leapt with joy! He had a bell at last!

And so, as the little bell went the rounds of the city with the little orphan boy, she pealed happily calling to the children: "Twangg-a-lang-langg! Mario is here! Sweet ice-cream for you! Twangg-a-lang-langgg!"

And when the little boys and girls came running, their happy, eager faces welcoming Mario and the bell, she sang louder still with a heart almost bursting with joy: "Why, this is wonderful! This is even better than singing from the heights of the church tower for here I am right among the people, close enough to see their happy faces! Twangg-a-lang-langgg! A Merry Christmas to all!"

II. IFUGAO TALES*

THE FIRE IN THE SKY

The gods were very happy about their new acquisition of fire. "Now," they declared, "we can cook all our meat and make it tastier!" The major gods and goddesses, the minor gods and goddesses, and the lesser gods and goddesses who were gathered around the fire, all nodded in agreement. They heaped lavish praises on it and wondered at its living power. The fire leaped higher and higher as, heady with the praises of the gods, it tried to show them its might.

Suddenly with a loud roar, it caught Bugan's low roof and soon it was dancing to and fro over the housetop. As it reduced Bugan's roof to embers, it executed a beautiful high jump to another goddess' roof and soon was dancing merrily on its heights, gathering force as it enveloped the whole house.

All the gods and goddesses were alarmed. At first, they fought the fire with their bare hands but soon got bruised and burned. Then they beat it with wooden sticks and bamboo poles, but these only added to the fire's strength. Soon terrified cries for help were heard from the seven rungs of heaven. Faint hearted gods and goddesses scampered about seeking places of safety while the more courageous ones continued to wage battle with the frightening menace.

On the earth below, the people viewed the reddening sky with increasing alarm. But Kabbigat and Ballitok, who had just returned from the Skyworld, assuaged their fears. "The gods are only cooking their meals," Kabbigat told them, "and, as gods will, they always do everything in a grand way.

"We have just returned from the Skyworld and we gave the gods fire in exchange for their rice," added Ballitok.

But soon the heat on earth became unbearable and when Kabbigat and Ballitok looked at the sky again, a portion of it seemed to be aflame! When they heard the cries for help, they knew something had gone wrong and made haste back to the Skyworld, bringing with them water and some blankets.

Upon reaching the sky regions, the brothers went to work at once. Again and again, they doused the flames with water and applied the water-soaked heavy blankets to them.

Finally, the fire was extinguished; only the smouldering embers of what once were houses glowed uncertainly in the soot-covered sky. Some of the gods were for returning the fire to the earthlings, but most of them wanted to retain it.

Kabbigat and Ballitok taught the gods how to contain the fire safely. They built a low structure and filled it with sand and soil. In the middle of this, they placed a tripod made from three medium-sized rocks which, they told the gods, would support their cooking pots. Over this structure, Kabbigat and Ballitok constructed a chimney through which the smoke could escape, assuring for the gods fresh air inside their houses while cooking.

The gods were profuse with their thanks to the two brothers. Before they returned to the earth-world, the gods gave them seedlings of the mongo beans which they were told to plant on earth and which now grow abundantly in Ifugaoland.

Kabbigat and Ballitok lived for a long time and the gods never failed to help them in their times of need.

— **From an Ifugao tale**

THE STAR MAIDEN

On a clear, cloudless night, when the sky seems studded with a thousand twinkling jewels, one can find three stars grouped together. Not far away, yet seemingly alone, is a bigger and brighter star. Beliefs of the Ifugao have it that these four stars are sisters and that the fourth and brightest one is the Star Maiden that once in the long ago, had lived in their land and married one of their tribesmen.

Once there was a rich man who owned a ricefield. Every night, when his rice plants were growing, he would visit his field to check the water that nourished his plants. He himself had built the waterway that coursed the water to his field from the spring nearby.

One night, he heard the laughing voices of young girls and the sound seemed to come from the pool that had formed around the spring. He thought his ears were playing tricks on him, but the giggling and the laughter persisted, so, with stealth, he approached the spring. There he saw four beautiful maidens enjoying themselves, splashing water at each other and squealing with delight. After a while, tiring of their game, the four lovely girls got out of the water to put on their tapis* which they had hidden among the bushes near the water's edge. Then, using their tapis as wings, the four maidens flew back to the sky. The surprised man immediately realized that the bathers were really stars.

The next night, the man was back in his field and again the same spectacle happened: the four girls were there once more, their peals of laughter reverberating through the quiet evening air.

The rich man looked more closely and while he saw that all four were beautiful, one stood out from all the rest. She was less boisterous than the others, standing a bit shyly away from the rest as they frolicked in the pool, and she had the most expressive eyes of all and the whitest, smoothest skin.

It was a sad man who watched the girls fly back to the sky that night for he had fallen deeply in love with the loveliest of them and he had no way of knowing if he would ever see her again.

On the third night, on a hunch, he went back to the pool and hid himself among the bushes near the water's edge. Presently, he heard the lively chatter of the girls as they came to the pool. One by one, they took off their tapis as they dove into the clear water. Happily, the rich man noted that the girl he loved had placed her tapis near the bush where he was hidden. While the girls were enjoying their swimming, he stole the tapis of the loveliest one and hid it inside his bamboo flute which he quickly tucked in his belt. He quickly disappeared to find another hiding place.

When it was time to go, the girls got back their tapis as usual, but one of them could not find hers. She searched and searched for it to no avail. Finally, her sisters told her that they could no longer wait for her for the night was coming to an end and they had to be back home. In tears, the loveliest one was left behind for she had no wings to fly with to take her back to the sky.

From behind his hiding place, the rich man appeared. In kind tones, he asked the girl why she was in such despair. The young maiden informed him that she had lost her tapis taking care not to reveal that she used it as wings to fly back to the sky.

"I'll give you another one if you will marry me," the rich man offered. The distraught girl did not tell him it was a special kind of tapis but kept quiet and followed the man to his home.

After some years of marriage, a child was born to the couple. When

---

* short, tube-like skirt

the child began to run about, the rich man admonished his wife: "Our child can play with anything in the house, but on no condition should you allow him to play with my bamboo flute!"

His wife agreed without question and kept the flute away from the child.

One day, however, when the father was out in the fields, the boy found the flute. He blew into it but no sound came. He tried to blow harder but the sound seemed to be trapped inside by something. He peered into the hole and bit by bit, he extracted a piece of fine cloth from inside the flute.

"Look what I found inside this flute, Mother! No wonder there was no sound when I blew on it!" and he pulled out the rest of the fine material from the flute. The material turned out to be his mother's long-lost tapis.

With her tapis back in her possession, the maiden knew she had to return to her real home in the sky. With a sad look, she kissed her son good-bye and winged her way back skywards.

The rich man was much grieved when he learned that his wife had left her earth-home for her home in the sky. But he comforted himself by looking at the sky on clear, cloudless evenings and seeing his wife there with her other star sisters. To him, she was the brightest and most beautiful star of all!

— **From an Ifugao folktale**

THE ORIGIN OF MOUNTAINS, HILLS, VALLEYS, AND THE SEAS

In the old days, the Middle World or the earth was flat and plain. There were no mountains or hills as we have them today. The earth was used mainly by the people of the Upperworld or Skyworld as a hunting ground, for its forests teemed with all kinds of wild animals. Hunting was the favorite pastime of the Skyworld people.

One day, Wigan, greatest of hunters, looked down from the Skyworld. He saw that it was a bright and sunny day. The wind was low and the trees scarcely moved their heads. It was a perfect time for hunting.

With his dogs, his hunting spear, and his *bango* or hunting bag, he descended to the earth-world.

Soon the bright rays of the sun penetrated the thick foliage of trees to the hiding places of the wild animals and Wigan's dogs began to smell them out from their hidden nooks. Suddenly, a wild pig darted away and at once the leader dog was after him, followed by the rest of the pack.

Wigan followed but could not overtake them. He called for his dogs, but they could not hear him as they seemed to be miles and miles away. He decided to get some rest, thinking, "My dogs are so occupied with catching that pig they cannot hear my call."

After a while, he took to the trail once more. He listened for the dogs' barking but heard none at all. He cupped his hand around his ears to hear better, but the sound he heard was so feeble and weak that he could not decide whether it was only the wind or the faint barking of his dogs. This enraged him.

"If there were mountains and hills to catch the sound and convey them back to me, I would know where my dogs are now." Again and again he called for his dogs and each time he was answered only by the silent winds.

"I am sure they have gone on to Kay-ang (the present town of Kiangan)," Wigan said, starting on the trail towards the place.

Soon he saw the birds returning to their nests and heard the wind hissing among the trees. Nightfall came but none of his dogs reappeared. Under the forest trees, he rested for the night while a plan that had been in his mind for days now finally took shape.

The next morning, he started for *Lagud* or the East. There he found the river that supplied all the waters of the earth. With his bango or hunting bag, he plugged the outlet and soon the waters got higher. It rose higher and higher and pretty soon he saw that *Dava* or the West was already flooded. He smiled to himself.

Then he looked towards Kay-ang. The waters made the village look like a huge lake shimmering in the sun. Still the waters rose.

As he looked at the rising waters, he asked himself, "What will happen next? If the waters rise any higher will they not reach the Skyworld? "

Wigan knew that water has no heart. It destroys everything that crosses its path. If it flooded the Upperworld, he knew he would get blamed for it.

Immediately he dove into the waters. Down, down to the river-source where he had placed his hunting bag to block its outward flow he swam. With all the strength he could muster he pulled at the *bango* until at last it gave way.

Like a thousand stampeding cattle, the great volume of water roared, rolled, and rushed downward where it emptied into what we now call the sea. When the waters in Kay-ang had drained at last, Wigan saw that mountains, hills and valleys had been formed.

From then on, Wigan enjoyed hunting in the earth-world. He easily caught the wild pigs which were no match for his dogs at mountain climbing. Also, he could clearly hear the dogs' barking as they pursued their prey up and down the mountainsides. He never lost a hunting dog after that. But the happiest result was that he and the Skyworld people fed on meat every day from that time on.

— **Based on an Ifugao tale**

WHY THE GABI LEAVES DO NOT GET WET

In the golden days, there lived a beautiful maiden in a small hut near a river. She loved plants and there was a profuse growth of flowers and other plants in her garden. Every day she would fetch water from the river for her plants.

In the river lived a river-fairy, and every day he saw the beautiful maiden as she came to fetch water. "Oh, what a beautiful maiden! " the river fairy exclaimed to himself. "And so kind and loving to her plants."

The river-fairy fell in love with the girl and one day, as she stood by the river bank to get water, he appeared to her. "Beautiful maiden, pray hear me. Every day I see you coming here to fetch water for your lovely flowers and plants to which you give such loving care. I have fallen in love with you. Will you love me as much and be my wife? "

"Oh, water-fairy," the girl replied, "I am a mortal and you are a fairy. How can I ever learn to love you? "

The river-fairy insisted, "You may not love me now but someday you may learn to return my love. . ."

"Such love is impossible," the girl argued.

"Nothing is impossible if you do not make it so," the river-fairy said. "I shall be waiting for your answer." And he named a date when he would return and claim her for his bride.

The beautiful maiden was sad for she did not love the river-fairy and he had hinted that he would not accept a negative answer. But as the months passed she forgot about the water-fairy and dismissed the whole incident as a bad dream.

It was summertime again. The bright sun made the flowers in the garden of the beautiful girl bloom and beam with the special radiance that only sun-kissed plants have. The maiden was just as radiant as her well-cared for plants. She sang them a happy song.

Down by the river, somebody was also singing happily. And his words, carried upriver by the gentle breezes, were: "Tomorrow, wedding bells will ring for my beloved and me. Tomorrow I will claim my bride."

At the exact hour that he had promised the maiden he would return, the river-fairy appeared. He was handsomely attired in wedding garments.

Again, he asked for the beautiful maiden's hand in marriage. Just as adamantly, the girl refused. "I gave you my answer last time and it hasn't changed."

The river-fairy could not believe that a mere mortal would refuse to marry him. His pride was hurt and in his fury he told the girl: "So you don't want to marry me, Beautiful Maiden? Well, neither can you marry anyone else! Since you love plants I shall transform you into a plant. But you shall be a plant that cannot drink water through its leaves for your leaves will never get wet. Unless your hard heart softens and you consent to be my wife, you shall remain a *gabi* plant forever and your leaves shall never know the coolness of rain nor drink of its refreshing water! "

So the beautiful maiden was transformed into a gabi plant. According to the Ifugao folks, it seems that she still refuses to marry the river-fairy for until now the gabi leaves do not get wet.

— **From an Ifugao tale**

WHY THE SKY IS HIGH

The Ifugaos live in the mountains of Northern Luzon, Philippines. They number about 100,000 in population. They are famous the world over for their remarkable rice terraces which look like giant steps reaching up to the skies. This story is their explanation of how the sky got its present height.

In the early days when the world was young, the sky was close to the earth. Every now and then the gods, who lived in the sky, would come down to earth to teach the people some religious rites or to attend their feasts. At the same time, the ancestors had only to climb the mountain peaks to reach the Skyworld in order to talk to the gods or to ask them some favors.

This arrangement, however, had one disadvantage — the gods of war, the powerful Manaha-uts, were fond of eating people and they would kill as many as they could get. Since the sky was so close to the earth, the Manaha-uts had only to look down from their sky-balcony to see who was giving birth and immediately, they would snatch away the soul of the new-born baby, leaving it dead. Or they would search for their victims on the lonely mountain trails or upon the high rice-terrace walls and push them off the steep heights to their deaths below. At other times, they would encourage people to go on the war-path against their enemies so that they, the Manaha-uts, could kill as many as they wanted on just one single occasion.

The people on earth began to fear that they would all be killed and the human race become extinct. Finally, they decided to appeal to the Maknongans, the gods of reproduction, who were more kindly disposed to the people. Sacrifices of pigs and chickens were offered to these gods to stop the Manaha-uts from their murderous game.

The chief Maknongan was seated on his haunches as was his wont. He shook his enormous head, sending the high winds scurrying to the east and west and the clouds careening in fright to the farthest corner of the sky.

"Those Manaha-uts are a stupid lot," he said. "Don't they realize that if they kill all the people no one will be left to offer sacrifices of pigs and chickens to us gods anymore?" But all he did was to curse the Manaha-uts.

The people on earth offered larger sacrifices and celebrated a big feast with gongs and dancing in honor of the Maknongan gods. The chief Maknongan was very pleased.

One day, when the Manaha-uts were at their gruesome game again and the wails and cries of the bereaved families were so loud that their din disturbed the gods in the sky, the chief Maknongan finally decided to put a stop to the wanton killing. He sent a go-between, an emissary god, to negotiate with the war-gods. The latter, however, just ignored the emissary-god and went on their merry, murderous way.

The chief Maknongan was greatly enraged. His enormous bulk seemed to grow into even more monstrous proportions as his fury mounted. Suddenly, he stood up from his sitting position and reached to his full height. A great crack was heard and the sky rose as Maknongan's enormous head and gigantic shoulders pushed it higher and higher away from the earth until it reached its present height today.

After that, the Manaha-uts could no longer reach the people so easily and fewer deaths occurred. Thus the Ifugaos have become more and more numerous.

— **Based on several Ifugao beliefs pieced together by the author**

WHY THE MOON LACKS BRILLIANCE

Long ago, the Sun and the Moon were very good friends. They always did things together, whether they were hunting wild game or attending feasts. But this friendship was not to last long for the Moon began to be boastful and proud.

"Look how important I am to the people on earth," he boasted one day, while the two of them were taking a promenade in the sky. "When they plant their crops they depend on me — they always wait till I give them the go-signal — which can hardly be said for you."

Another time, the Moon was at it again. "Look how handsome I am! People always look at me with admiration in their eyes. But when they look at you they squint and frown, or close their eyes. They cannot stand your ugly face." And he looked down at the great ocean below to see his handsome reflection in the waters.

The Sun stood this boasting and self-praise for some time but his silence was taken by the Moon as agreement, and the latter grew worse day by day.

"Look how the people on earth love me! When I appear in the sky they all come out to play or hold dance-fests or just bask under my pure white brilliance. But when it is you they see, why, they all seem to run away, going under trees or houses just to hide from you! "

Finally, the Sun had had enough of Moon's boastfulness. What he deplored was not that Moon was constantly praising himself, for if he had that high an opinion of himself, that was his business. What Sun did not like was that every time Moon praised himself to high heavens, he would drag Sun's name into the mire. So Sun decided to put a stop to it.

One day, Sun told Moon that he was going away for a while. Moon agreed, saying, "It would be a good change for you." But what he really meant was that he, Mr. Moon, would enjoy being alone for a change, for he thought that the Sun was jealous of him and was less companionable a friend that he had been before.

As soon as the Moon was out of sight, Sun changed himself into a beautiful rainbow. The rainbow then went to a river from whose banks she gathered sea shells. Collecting the shells into a heap, she built a fire and burned them to make lime. After the fire had cooled, she gathered the white powdery ashes or lime and placed them in her hip-bag. Then the rainbow returned to the sky and changed herself into the Sun once again.

That day there was a big feast at Nundaol, or the Underworld, to which both Sun and Moon were invited. As usual, they decided to go together.

When they arrived, the feast was already in progress. The Moon, who enjoyed drinking rice wine and was inclined to drunkenness, sat himself near the rice-wine jars where a lot of people, similarly inclined, were gathered. The Sun, who was planning his revenge, abstained from the strong-kicking *baya* juice and moved away to where other guests were dancing. As he walked away, he heard Moon begin his usual opener:

"Look how important I am to the people on earth. . .! " Pretty soon, Sun knew, a full-blown boasting session would ensue around the rice-wine jars when tongues would be loosened by the effects of the wine.

The feast progressed with no unlikely incidents, for those who indulged in the rice wine around the jars were too drunk to stand up and fight. Moon, in fact, was so inebriated that he fell asleep.

Soon the feast was over and everybody started to go home. Sun looked for Moon and roused him from his sleep. "It is time to go. All the other guests have left."

But the Moon was still feeling drowsy from the wine and told Sun, "Go ahead, don't wait for me. I shall follow later."

"All right then, but be careful when you reach Habiatan." Sun was sport enough to warn his friend of impending danger at the fork where the crossroads that separated the Skyworld from the Underworld converged.

Then he hurried on to execute his plans. When he reached Habiatan, he tied the bag of lime to a tree under which he knew Moon would have to pass.

When the Moon woke up, he was a bit refreshed. Taking his spear, he sang along the way, swinging it up and down. "Oh, what a great one I am, a great one I am! " he sang in a tuneless monotone.

Upon reaching Habiatan, he remembered Sun's warning. He looked all around him and approached the site cautiously. He soon filled the air with ripples of laughter for he saw only a bag hanging from a branch of the tree which stood at the crossroads. "Hah, Mr.

Sun is certainly nervous these days," he laughed. "Imagine, being afraid of a mere bag hanging from a tree! " and he doubled up in a fit of laughter.

Presently, he went under the branch that held the bag and with his spear tried to unloose the bag. When he could not detach it from the branch, he lunged at the bag with his spear with such force that the bag was ripped open and all the lime spilled on him, pouring on his eyes and face with its acid power.

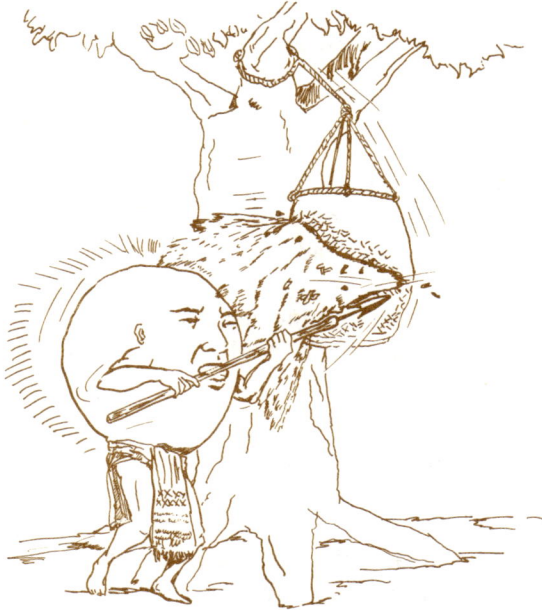

"Help! Help! " Moon's pitiful cries brought his sons *Bala-a* or Venus, *Pawit* the small Dipper, and *Talao*, the Morning Star, to his side. They wiped off the lime from his eyes and face, but some of the lime-ash stuck permanently and could not be taken off.

Thus did the Moon lose some of his brilliance.

THE MOON'S REVENGE,

or

Why We Have Eclipses

Mr. Moon was not likely to forget Mr. Sun's despicable trick and he secretly made plans for his revenge. The opportunity for this took a long time in coming — which made Sun believe that all was forgiven — but finally it did come.

Another big feast was announced at *Nundaol,* or the Underworld, which invitation both of them readily accepted. As usual, they journeyed together.

At the feast, Mr. Sun drank freely of the wine, egged on by Moon who pretended to take generous sips of the powerful rice-wine, although, in truth, he wasn't drinking at all for he had certain plans in mind.

Pretty soon, the strong-kicking wine loosened Mr. Sun's tongue and he began to brag about how he had taught the boastful Moon a lesson. This was just what the Moon had wanted to hear — a self-admission from the Sun of the lime-bag trick the latter had played on him.

When the feast was over and all the guests were leaving, the Moon roused the Sun from his drunken stupor. "Let's start on our way for the feast is over."

But the Sun had a very bad hang-over and decided to sleep it off some more. "Just go ahead and I shall follow later," he told Moon, which was just what the Moon desired.

"All right, then, I will go ahead of you. But be very careful when you reach Habiatan," he mouthed exactly the same warning that Sun had given him before. The Sun thanked Moon, then immediately went back to sleep.

The Moon skipped happily towards Habiatan singing a song: "Be careful now, Sun, for I am just paying back the debt I owe you. Sweet is revenge! "

At the fork where the two roads met, one of which led to the Skyworld and the other to the Underworld, he dug a very deep hole similar to that which the earth-people used in trapping wild pigs. He knew Sun would use this path in going to the Skyworld. Over the top of the hole, he placed a rotten log over which he laid a piece of rope which was really a noose. All these he cleverly covered with grass so no one would ever suspect there was a trap.

He tied the other end of the rope, which he disguised to look like a hanging vine, to a high branch of the same tree Mr. Sun had used before for his bag of lime. Moon also hung a bag similar to the lime-bag of Mr. Sun.

Soon Mr. Sun woke up. He felt at the top of the world. Nothing seemed to dampen his spirits, not even the suspicion that Moon was cooking up something against him, for he had decided that he was not going to fall into any trap laid by Moon.

Upon reaching Habiatan, he walked cautiously and looked for signs of trouble. But he saw only the bag hanging from the tree by the fork. The sight sent him into fits of hysterical laughter. "Does that stupid Moon think I will fall into the same trap?" and he laughed even louder.

He relaxed his guard and carelessly walked towards the trap that Moon had laid for him. Suddenly, the ground fell from under him and he was catapulted into the air. The noose was suddenly around his neck, and while it began to tighten, he fell unconscious, hanging helplessly in mid-air.

Down on earth, the bright day was suddenly turned to night. The people hurried from their fields. There was much confusion and some people lost their way for they could not find the mountain paths in the darkness. Mothers gathered their children, some of whom were crying, afraid of the sudden gloom.

The roosters were confused, too. They did not know whether to sing their waking-up songs or the goodnight songs. There was indeed a cackle of argument about it and many of them just sang any which way:

Toook- to-ga-ooookkkk!

Ga-ok- toookkkk!

But the little chickens did not seem to care — they just went back to sleep again.

Soon all the people were gathered in the village square which was now lighted with torches made from pine branches wet with pitch. Everybody who had musical instruments brought out their gongs, *pattungs, bangibangs.* and drums, for the priests and the wise old men told them to make a loud noise to wake the Sun up. Priests offered sacrifices of hastily caught pigs and chickens to their ancestors to intervene and ask the Sun to show his brilliant face again. At the same time, all the people shouted at the Sun:

"Wake up, wake up! Shine again! "

The Sun was encouraged by the support given him; with one supreme effort, he broke the rope that had started to cut into his neck and strangle him. Then, in all his former splendor, he shone again.

All the people on earth rejoiced when the Sun began to shine again. They danced and feasted for three days.

Hearing all the shouts of jubilation and the happy din of their musical instruments, the Sun remarked to the Moon: "See how much the people on earth miss me even when I just sleep for a little while? "

But the Moon just went away vowing he would get back at the Sun again some day. According to the Ifugao folks, that is why we have eclipses or why, occasionally, night comes even in the midst of bright sunlit days.

THE TALE OF THE PORCELAIN JARS

In Ifugao can be found many beautiful Chinese porcelain jars, some dating back to the 12th century. These are used as containers for the rice-wine which is used in their religious rites. As with everything that has a ritual function for this people, supernatural origins are attributed to the jars.

Bangilit was a *Kadangyan,* or rich man, who owned four rice granaries and a very large house. He was not a priest so he was able to indulge in his favorite pastime, hunting.

Every year, after harvest time, when his rice was finally stored in the granary and the religious rites for its safekeeping and its miraculous increase had been prayed for by the priests, he would pack his hunting bag, get his hunting spear from its hiding place, and, with his dogs, leave for his favorite hunting grounds.

On one of these hunting trips, he was benighted in the forest. He called for his dogs but they were nowhere in sight, so he decided to rest and take his evening meal. He built a fire, cooked, and ate.

Presently, one of the dogs appeared. After giving it food, Bangilit put it on leash and let it lead him home. Somewhere in the deep forest they found a path. The dog barked. At some distance away an answering bark was heard which Bangilit thought came from his other dog. So they kept to the same path and went on hoping to find the other dog.

Soon, the dog with him began to whine, then strain at its leash, so that it was all Bangilit could do to keep up with the dog. For a while, his dog kept Bangilit on a half-run. Suddenly, they came upon a very brightly lighted place, where a large group of people were gathered.

"Surely, Bangilit is dead," he heard one of them say.

"Where were you speared?" another one queried, giving him a close scrutiny.

He looked at them but there seemed to be no one he recognized although they seemed to know his name. "I have not been speared nor am I dead," Bangilit assured them. "I was only hunting in the forest and was overtaken by night. Then my dog led me here and lo, it is light!"

They took Bangilit to their village which was really the dwelling place of the souls. They were very hospitable and offered him food which Bangilit politely refused, saying, "I still have some food in my hunting bag. When it is gone, then I shall ask for some."

In return for their hospitality, Bangilit helped his new friends in their work. Since it was harvest time he was with them from early morning to dusk, helping them harvest their rice crop. He worked well and they were pleased with him.

"How long do you expect to stay here with us? " one of them asked him.

"About four days," Bangilit replied. The people all laughed and told him that four days in the land of the souls was equal to four years on earth. Bangilit kept the information to himself and remained silent. Finally he requested permission to go home to his family for he had become very homesick.

Before he left, the souls gave him four porcelain jars which they said were a gift for they all liked the hardworking man. He thanked the souls and asked for directions home. They led him to a hole in the sky where a ladder was suspended.

"Use this ladder and keep going. In no time at all, you will reach your home."

As he started to descend, one of the jars, which he carried on his back tied with rattan twine around his shoulders, got loose and fell and broke. He told himself to be more careful and not to hurry so.

Finally he found himself on top of a betel-nut tree. He slid down its trunk and set foot on solid earth soil at last. As he stood there trying to peer beyond the darkness around him, he heard the roosters crow and he knew it was the coming of early dawn. When his eyes got used to the early dawn gloom, he was happily surprised to find himself in his very own house-yard.

"Who are you? " the people in his house did not readily recognize him.

"I am *Kadangyan* Bangilit and I own this house. Don't you recognize me at all? "

His relatives could not believe it, but when they looked closer, they saw it was indeed their long-lost relative. "We all thought you were dead! It is four years since you left for the hunt! "

"They also thought I was dead when I appeared at their place. They asked where I had been speared."

"Who? " his relatives wondered to whom he was referring.

"The souls in the Skyworld," Bangilit told them.

His relatives shook their heads and thought to themselves: surely, Bangilit is not in his right mind to imagine such things!

But when Bangilit showed them the jars he had brought, they were all amazed for nobody had ever owned such jars in their village. They had carvings of dragons, flowers, clouds and other patterns that could only belong to another world. They all began questioning him about their source.

"From the Skyworld, in the land of the souls," Bangilit said and he told them of the ladder that connected to the top of the betel-nut palm on which he had made his descent.

Everybody rushed outside to look for the ladder but it was no longer there. Only the betel-nut tree, with its graceful palms swaying in the early morning breeze and not quite reaching the clouds, stood there. And if it knew the secret of the ladder, it was not saying anything.

The Ifugao folks say, however, that the three jars that Bangilit brought are still in existence. According to them, one is owned by Binway of the village of Buwot; another by Inayaw of Hinagangan; and the third by Buwit of the village of Hapao. Maybe, one day, when you have a chance to go up to Ifugao, high up in the mountains of northern Luzon, you can inquire about these jars and see for yourself the jars that came from the land of the Souls in the Skyworld.

— **Adapted from an Ifugao tale recorded by Prof. Ottley Beyer.**

III. OTHER REGIONAL TALES*

15. **THE ORIGIN OF BOHOL ISLAND AND ITS PEOPLE**
    (Adapted from a Boholano tale)

16. **THE PUNISHMENT OF THE FISHTAIL PALM AND THE BURI PALM**
    (Adapted from a Visayan tale)

17. **THE ORIGIN OF THE RAINBOW**
    (Adapted from a Tagalog folktale)

18. **THE ADVENTURES OF JUAN PUSONG**

    a.   **JUAN AND THE CRABS**
    b.   **JUAN AND THE ICE-CANDY BAR**
    c.   **JUAN AND THE BAMBOO LADDER**

THE ORIGIN OF BOHOL ISLAND AND ITS PEOPLE

Bohol island, in the central part of the Philippines, is shaped like a turtle's back. The Boholanos have a tale to explain its origin.

Once upon a time, there were no people except those who lived in the sky. This was because there was no land for people to live on, there being only a huge vast ocean below the sky.

One day, the daughter of the chieftain in the sky fell ill and seemed to grow worse by the day. The most powerful medicine man of the village was sent for and after performing some divination rites, he told the chieftain that the only cure lay in the roots of a certain wild balete tree which, the medicine-man said, the girl must touch.

Soon after, the people in the sky began to dig around the tree in order to get at its roots. Since it was a very large tree, they dug for several days until at last they had exposed most of its roots. Then they lowered the sick girl into the pit they had dug so she could touch the roots and imbibe of their magic healing power.

Unfortunately, the people had dug the hole too deeply and the sick girl fell through the floor of the sky as the thin soil gave way. As she plunged through the air, two big birds saw the falling girl and caught her with their powerful wings from where she hung, helplessly suspended in mid-air.

A big turtle chanced upon the poor girl's plight and hastily called all the swimming animals to a meeting to save her. Big Turtle told everyone gathered that soil must be brought from the ocean's floor to create land in order to save the hapless girl. Then he asked the frog to undertake the mission.

The frog was gone but in a short time he returned without the needed soil. He admitted failure of his mission. Then Big Turtle called upon the mouse to do his best in getting the soil but Mouse had hardly dived into the waters when he surfaced again. He said the ocean was bottomless.

Finally, an old toad, whom nobody had even noticed was there, volunteered to get the dirt-soil from the ocean's depths. He was immediately turned down, his offer met with jeers and laughter, the loudest objections coming from those who had failed.

But Big Turtle, now getting desperate, was willing to try anyone who volunteered for the task, and sent Old Toad to the ocean's depths with his blessings.

Old Toad was gone for a long time but when he finally surfaced, he brought with him a few grains of sand. These he spread around Big Turtle's back and from this, according to the Boholanos, an island grew which today is called Bohol. The girl who had fallen from the sky lived on the island and from her all Boholanos have descended.

— Adapted from a Boholano tale

THE PUNISHMENT OF THE FISHTAIL PALM
AND THE BURI PALM

(Or Why the Fishtail-palm and Buri-palm Trees
Die After Bearing Fruits)

When the world was young, all the trees could talk and laugh and cry. Bathala, the supreme skyworld god, had created them just like men. They could walk about or run about in play, dancing in the wind or splashing in the rain. They cried when they got hurt or bled when they got wounded.

One day, men appeared on the earth. They looked around for shelter against the rain and the strong sun. At first, they lived inside caves, but as their number grew, the caves became too crowded. The people wanted some shelter where they could see the sun and listen to the rain or feel the refreshing wind on their faces. The caves were too dark even in the daytime and the air inside was hot and stale.

One day, the men began to cut down the trees to make houses. The poor trees cried and moaned in pain. More men came and more trees were decapitated, or worse, totally cut down or up-rooted. Soon there was a great cry from the trees to the god Bathala to spare them from further suffering. They entreated Bathala to stop the wholesale slaughter.

Bathala called all the trees together. He told them that men needed the trees for their houses and that he could not deny them these for men needed shelter from the elements. However, Bathala told the trees that he would take away their human characteristics and they would thenceforth feel no pain when men cut off their limbs and branches. He also granted them longer lives, far longer than those he had granted any of his creatures.

Unfortunately, while Bathala was talking, the Fishtail Palm and the Buri Palm-tree went on merrily chatting and talking to each other, ignoring the great Bathala himself and paying no attention to what he was telling them. This gross disrespect greatly angered the mighty sky-god and he told the two trees:

"Because you have not listened to me nor paid any attention to what has been said here, you two, unlike the other trees, shall not have the gift of long life. Instead, you shall die after you bear fruit."

Thus, while most trees live to a ripe old age, the Fishtail palm-tree and the Buri-palm tree die after they have borne fruit.

— Adapted from a Visayan tale

THE ORIGIN OF THE RAINBOW

In the early days of the world, it is said that there was no rainbow. This beautiful multi-colored arc that stretches from the earth to the sky was first used by Bathala, supreme lord of the sky and king of the gods and goddesses, as a bridge to connect the earth and heaven.

In those days, Bathala and the lesser gods and goddesses used to live on earth with the people. They taught the people how to hunt for food in the forest, how to raise food from the earth, how to make war, and how to cure illnesses.

One day, Bathala decided to visit his kingdom in the sky. He ordered to be brought to him his strong fine horse, which could jump over the mountains and could run as fast as the wind. Bathala's servants immediately mounted on its back the most beautiful saddle, made of fine leather and decorated with silver and gold. Bathala then informed his people where he was going and bade them all good-bye.

Bathala and his horse travelled to the ends of the earth until they reached a vast ocean. This was the most extreme point of the earth and had to be crossed in going to the sky. This place was also the nearest to the sky and on clear days one could hear the voices of the sky-people.

Bathala stopped his horse and in a loud voice called to his servants in the sky, ordering them to place a bridge so that he could pass through. Suddenly, a beautiful multi-colored bridge appeared in the sky, brightening Bathala's pathway.

Bathala's servants lowered one end of the bridge until it connected the earth to the sky. Over

this heavenly bridge Bathala spurred his horse, reaching heaven without further delay.

Since that time the rainbow has been called *balag-hari* or path-bridge of the king. Today, when people see the rainbow, they know that Bathala is again on his powerful horse, journeying from the earth to the sky, to visit his kingdom there.

— Adapted from a Tagalog folktale

THE ADVENTURES OF JUAN PUSONG

In many regions of the Philippines, there are many stories about the funny adventures of a dull, lazy boy. He goes by the name of *Juan Pusong* among the Visayans, *Juan Tamad* among the Tagalogs, *Pilanduk* among the Tiruray tribes in Mindanao, etc. These stories sometimes end tragically for Juan, but he never seems to learn from his sad experiences.

JUAN AND THE CRABS

One day, Juan was sent to the market by his mother to buy some crabs for their lunch. Juan took the basket his mother gave him to put the crabs in and went on his way.

At the market he selected five big crabs and placed them inside the basket, taking care to cover it securely as his mother told him to. He was about to return home when he passed by a group of boys. He sat down to watch and soon became fascinated with the game. Pretty soon he heard noises coming from the basket as the crabs began to clamber and crawl about seeking their freedom. This annoyed Juan and he lifted the cover of the basket and shouted to the crabs:

"So, you want to go home already? Impatient Ones! All right, you go ahead and tell mother I shall be right along! " He took the crabs out of the basket, set them on the ground and bade them hurry homeward.

It was almost noon when Juan returned to his home. He was very hungry and the thought of the delicious crabs for lunch brought water to his mouth.

"I shall have three big crabs and mother can have the other two. She will surely like that," he mused as he hastened his steps toward home.

But when Juan reached his house his mother was waiting for him at the door and she was very angry.

"Where are the crabs? It has been four hours since I sent you out to buy them! "

"Aren't they home yet? " Juan was genuinely surprised. "I sent them well ahead of me so that you could cook them! "

Juan's mother gave him a sound spanking that made him cry out: "Aray! Aray! You should spank the crabs, not me! " he protested.

The very next day, Juan went back to the market to look for the crabs. He was sore at the crabs and vowed to take revenge. He took the shorter route along the river-bank intent on finding a big stick to beat the crabs with. Just then he espied a big crab as it crawled into a hole in the sand.

"Aha! So you are trying to hide from me, eh? Where are your other companions? Are they hiding in that hole, too? " And he knelt near the hole and peered into its darkness.

"Come out, you cowards! Come out and take the same punishment I got yesterday because of you! " And he pummeled the hole with his bare hands. Pretty soon, a big claw snapped shut on two of his fingers. Juan shouted in pain to let go. To this day, Juan's two little fingers are much shorter than his other fingers for the crab had taken them away to punish Juan.

— A tale remembered from childhood.

JUAN AND THE ICE-CANDY BAR

One day, Juan journeyed to the city to look for work. While standing at a street corner he chanced upon an ice-cream vendor.

"Why are you ringing a bell? Are you a church?" he inquired of the vendor.

"I am selling ice-cream," replied the man.

Not knowing what it was, Juan asked to buy the cheapest one in the box. The vendor gave him an ice-candy bar. At his first taste, he jumped and his candy bar almost fell from his hand.

"You did not tell me it was cold!" he accused the vendor. "Are you trying to kill me?"

The vendor explained that the candy was made of ice and milk sweetened with sugar. Juan laughed and told the vendor it was his first visit to the city. Upon hearing this, the vendor gave Juan an extra bar of ice-candy as a present in honor of the occasion. Juan thanked the vendor but he did not eat the second bar. His teeth had become too numbed from eating the frozen candy so he decided to take it to his mother.

Juan placed the ice-candy bar inside his *tambayoyong* bag inside which were his few clothes he had packed for his stay in the city. In the late afternoon, finding no hope for employment, he journeyed back to his town. Excitedly, he related to his mother the new and strange sights he saw in the city. He told her also of the vendor with the bell.

Then he remembered his present and grandly announced to his mother the gift he brought for her from the big city.

"Close your eyes and put out your tongue like this," he told his mother. Then he took his tambayoyong and opened it but to his great disbelief and consternation, the ice-candy bar was gone. He searched for it among his clothes, taking each one of them out, but all he found was his wet clothes.

"Thief, thief! Someone has stolen my present for my mother. Thief, thief!" Juan cried at the top of his voice.

The neighbors all came running to the house attracted by the big noise made by Juan. They feared the worst.

"A thief has run off with my present for my mother!" Juan bewailed his loss and pointed to the opened tambayoyong.

"Look, the thieving rascal even urinated on my clothes!" And he showed them his damp clothes inside the tambayoyong.

But the neighbors all began to laugh, shaking their heads hopelessly at Juan when they learned that he had brought home an ice-candy bar and had tucked it among his clothes inside his tambayoyong.

— A tale remembered from childhood

JUAN AND THE BAMBOO LADDER

Once, when Juan went to another town, he got lost and could not find his way to a relative's house. Since it was well past noon, he accepted the invitation of a kindly old man for lunch at the latter's house.

On the dining table was a dish of young bamboo shoots. It was deliciously garnished with onions and tomatoes, and cooked in coconut milk. Juan had never tasted such a dish before and found it so much to his liking that he finished the whole dish without leaving any for his host.

"Oh, it is only from bamboo," the old man replied but did not elaborate as he was most displeased with his visitor's lack of manners.

When Juan got home, he asked his mother for his sharp bolo.

"Where are you going? " his mother asked.

"I am going to make some vegetable salad," replied Juan. He then proceeded to detach the bamboo ladder from the front entrance of their house and began to cut this into small pieces. He placed the pieces inside a big pot, added water, and put the pot over a fire to boil.

Needless to say, Juan and his mother never got to eat the bamboo dish he was preparing.

GLOSSARY

bangibang — musical instrument

bango — hunting bag

Dava — West

Habiatan — crossroads separating the Skyworld and the Underworld

haludag — death chair

Kabunian — Skyworld god who made the earth

kadangyan — rich man

Lagud — East

Maknongans — gods of reproduction

Manaha-uts — gods of war

mumbaki — priest-healer

Nundaol — Underworld

panon-acan — a special ricefield belonging to the rice-chief

pattung — musical instrument

tambayoyong — a woven elongated shopping basket usually made of a
    certain kind of palm leaf